SPECIAL REPORTS

THE SILENCE BREAKERS
AND THE #METOO
MOVEMENT

BY DUCHESS HARRIS, JD, PHD WITH REBECCA MORRIS

Essential Library

An Imprint of Abdo Publishing | abdobooks.com

abdobooks.com

Published by Abdo Publishing, a division of ABDO, PO Box 398166, Minneapolis,
Minnesota 55439. Copyright © 2019 by Abdo Consulting Group, Inc. International
copyrights reserved in all countries. No part of this book may be reproduced in
any form without written permission from the publisher. Essential Library™ is a
trademark and logo of Abdo Publishing.

Printed in the United States of America, North Mankato, Minnesota
092018
012019

Cover Photo: Stephanie Keith/Getty Images News/Getty Images
Interior Photos: Rebecca Droke/Pittsburgh Post-Gazette/AP Images, 4–5; Lev
Radin/Shutterstock Images, 9; J. Stone/Shutterstock Images, 10; Matt Slocum/AP
Images, 16–17; Picture History/Newscom, 18–19; AP Images, 20; Scott Andersen/AP
Images, 25; Pablo Martinez Monsivais/AP Images, 27; Ted S. Warren/AP Images, 32;
Craig Ruttle/AP Images, 35; Andrey_Popov/Shutterstock Images, 36–37; Matt York/
AP Images, 41; Dia Dipasupil/Vanity Fair/Getty Images Entertainment/Getty Images,
45; iStockphoto, 46–47, 54; Tina Fineberg/AP Images, 50; Rebecca Cook/Reuters/
Newscom, 56–57; Carlos Osorio/AP Images, 59; Kathy Willens/AP Images, 63; Dale
G. Young/Detroit News/AP Images, 66; Mark Ralston/AFP/Getty Images, 68–69;
Susan Montoya Bryan/AP Images, 73; Corey Perrine/AP Images, 75; Taylor Jewell/
Invision/AP Images, 78–79; Erik McGregor/Pacific Press/LightRocket/Getty Images,
84; Damian Dovarganes/AP Images, 88–89; Star Shooter/MediaPunch/Ipx/AP Images,
90–91; Jordan Strauss/Invision/AP Images, 95; Sundry Photography/Shutterstock
Images, 99

Editor: Alyssa Krekelberg
Series Designer: Maggie Villaume

Library of Congress Control Number: 2018948251

Publisher's Cataloging-in-Publication Data

Names: Harris, Duchess, author. | Morris, Rebecca, author.
Title: The silence breakers and the #MeToo movement / by Duchess Harris and
        Rebecca Morris.
Description: Minneapolis, Minnesota : Abdo Publishing, 2019 | Series: Special
        reports set 4 | Includes online resources and index.
Identifiers: ISBN 9781532116834 (lib. bdg.) | ISBN 9781532159671 (ebook)
Subjects: LCSH: Sexual harassment--United States--Juvenile literature. | Sexual
        assault--Juvenile literature. | Mass media--Social aspects--United States--
        Juvenile literature. | Social problems in mass media--Juvenile literature.
Classification: DDC 305.42--dc23

CONTENTS

Chapter One
THE STORY OF #METOO   4

Chapter Two
BEFORE #METOO   18

Chapter Three
#METOO IN THE WORKPLACE   36

Chapter Four
THE MOVEMENT OUTSIDE OF WORK   46

Chapter Five
MINORS IN THE MOVEMENT   56

Chapter Six
THE #METOO MOVEMENT AND RACE   68

Chapter Seven
GENDER AND SEXUAL ORIENTATION   78

Chapter Eight
THE PAST AND FUTURE   90

Essential Facts   100
Glossary   102
Additional Resources   104

Source Notes   106
Index   110
About the Authors   112

CHAPTER ONE

THE STORY OF
#METOO

n 1997, community activist Tarana Burke was working at a youth camp in Alabama. The camp was for girls of color from poor and low-income homes. Many of the girls had experienced some form of neglect or abuse. The counselors encouraged the girls to share their stories in group discussions and privately with adults. One day, a 13-year-old girl named Heaven approached Burke. Heaven told Burke about the sexual abuse she suffered at the hands of her mother's boyfriend. Heaven's story was so disturbing that Burke could only manage to listen for a few minutes before sending Heaven to another counselor. As Heaven walked away, Burke remembers how she felt: "I watched

Tarana Burke has spent years advocating for people of color.

her put her mask back on and go back into the world like she was all alone."[1]

Burke is also a survivor of sexual assault. For several years, Burke reflected on that day with Heaven. She realized how much it would have mattered to say simply "me too" so that Heaven would know she was not alone. Burke calls this concept "empowerment through empathy."[2] In 2006, Burke started a page on the social media site Myspace. She wanted the page to be an outlet for survivors, especially those from marginalized communities, to share their stories. Burke promoted the phrase "me too" on the page. Thousands of women added their experiences in response. Even so, the phrase remained relatively unknown.

A VIRAL MOMENT

The phrase gained widespread, national attention in October 2017. Actress Alyssa Milano used it on Twitter to promote awareness about sexual harassment, abuse, and assault. In the tweet, Milano wrote, "If you've been sexually harassed or assaulted write 'me too' as a reply to this tweet."[3] Within 24 hours, people had used the term in statuses and replies millions of times. On Facebook alone, the term appeared in more than 12 million posts and reactions.[4]

Milano's message came just days after the *New York Times* published an article about Harvey Weinstein, a prominent movie, television, and play producer. The article showed Weinstein as a serial sexual predator. The revelation conflicted with his public image as the force behind many well-known films. For more than 30 years, Weinstein had been one of the most powerful and influential men in the arts and entertainment industry. With his brother Bob, he founded the successful production companies Miramax and the Weinstein Company. The companies produced

A SHOCKING DISCONNECT

Allegations against prominent figures named in the #MeToo movement can be shocking. That's because these figures are familiar to their victims and to the general public. Many people knew and respected Weinstein's work. He shaped movie experiences for millions of viewers. As a result, the allegations resonated deeply even with those who did not know Weinstein personally.

The same holds true for accusations against leaders in other industries. In the case of media figures, people may have a particular sense of familiarity. That's because people see these media figures every day, broadcast on screens in their homes. For example, Matt Lauer anchored a daily morning show. He also hosted traditional, sentimental events such as the Macy's Thanksgiving Day Parade. Viewers felt comfortable with him and liked him. NBC fired Lauer in November 2017 after several women made reports of his sexually inappropriate behavior. Afterward, there was a shocking disconnect between the familiar figure people thought they knew and the exposed perpetrator.

acclaimed films including *Pulp Fiction*, *Shakespeare in Love*, *Good Will Hunting*, *Chicago*, and *Silver Linings Playbook*, as well as popular franchises such as *Scary Movie* and *Scream*. These films helped to advance the careers of many actors, including Gwyneth Paltrow, Matt Damon, Ben Affleck, and Jennifer Lawrence.

In all, the films Weinstein produced or distributed earned more than 300 Academy Award nominations and more than 80 wins.[5] Weinstein has also won Tony Awards for his work on Broadway plays. He's also produced popular television series such as *Project Runway*. In his work, Weinstein addressed serious issues of sex and gender. He also said he was an advocate of humanitarian causes, including women's rights.

Because of Weinstein's work and public image, the *New York Times* article was shocking to many people. The piece described Weinstein's pattern of sexual harassment and assault on women across almost three decades. Weinstein would arrange private meetings with female employees, actors, and hopeful professionals. Then he would offer career assistance while making unwanted sexual advances. The behavior ranged from soliciting massages to rape.

Harvey Weinstein faced multiple felony charges.

In the week after the *New York Times* article ran, more than 60 women shared their experiences of harassment by Weinstein.[6] In the months that followed, others added their voices. Weinstein was fired from his own production company. Members of the Academy of Motion Picture Arts and Sciences voted to expel him from the organization. In May 2018, Weinstein was charged with rape and turned himself in to police. Weinstein posted bail and pleaded not guilty to the charges. A judge required him to turn over his passport and wear an electronic monitoring device while the case was ongoing.

The exposure of such an influential figure had a strong ripple effect. Soon, accusations came against people at the top of their fields in many industries. *Today Show* host Matt

Matt Lauer was accused of sexually harassing and assaulting his female coworkers.

Lauer, Minnesota senator Al Franken, Olympic gymnastics team doctor Larry Nassar, celebrity chef Mario Batali, Metropolitan Opera conductor James Levine, actor Kevin Spacey, and many others were accused. Most of these figures resigned or were fired. Some are facing criminal charges and civil lawsuits.

BREAKING SILENCE

The Weinstein scandal sparked a discussion about why it took so long for many of the women to share their stories of his harassment. People also questioned why it took so long for the news to break and for the story to gather attention. Some of the women abused by Weinstein felt powerless to step forward and report the incidents to anyone. Some felt guilty, confused, or afraid. They also feared the effect that reports would have on their careers.

Weinstein was one of the most influential people in the industry. The women he targeted were typically young and just beginning their careers. Some women confided only in close friends without making official police reports. When women did report the harassment and abuse to colleagues or to people at Weinstein's companies,

WHY PEOPLE STAY SILENT

Researchers consistently emphasize that sexual harassment and sexual violence are underreported. People remain silent for many reasons. Those reasons vary with factors such as age, race, economic status, gender, and sexual orientation. One of the most common reasons for silence is victim blaming. Victim blaming suggests that victims bring abuse upon themselves. Examples of victim blaming include criticizing a victim for wearing a revealing outfit or asking why a victim did not fight back. Another common reason for silence is fear of reprisal. Reprisal refers to retaliation through attacks on a victim's physical well-being, job, or reputation. A third common reason for silence is concern for the perpetrator. If the perpetrator is someone the victim knows, the victim may worry about the consequences the perpetrator could face. Some survivors remain silent because they do not want anyone to know about the harassment or abuse. Some people fear that no one will believe them.

Weinstein took actions to stop the spread of their stories. He paid settlements, and in return the women had to sign nondisclosure agreements. These agreements stopped them from ever speaking about Weinstein's behavior. Weinstein thus created and enforced what *New York Times* journalists Jodi Kantor and Megan Twohey called "a code of silence."[7] The women who spoke out against Weinstein—and the women and men who have spoken out against other perpetrators of sexual harassment and abuse—are now known as the silence breakers.

To continue discussions around the Weinstein case and others, Milano tweeted in October 2017, "If all the women who have been sexually harassed or assaulted wrote

'Me too' as a status, we might give people a sense of the magnitude of the problem."[8] Social media users began to reply using a hashtag before the phrase. Hashtags categorize posts by topic. Users can click or tap on the hashtag to view other posts and replies on the topic. Hashtags also allow social media platforms to analyze how popular a topic is.

The hashtag #MeToo quickly went viral. Soon, people made the connection to Burke's earlier use of the phrase. Milano was not aware of Burke's existing Me Too movement when she began her social media campaign. Instead, Milano's message was rooted in her own experiences as well as those of her acquaintances. For example, Milano's friend, actress Rose McGowan, was one of the women who accused Weinstein of rape. Milano communicated with Burke once she learned of the earlier campaign. The movement then become an opportunity for various advocacy efforts to intersect.

"THIS RECKONING APPEARS TO HAVE SPRUNG UP OVERNIGHT. BUT IT HAS ACTUALLY BEEN SIMMERING FOR YEARS, DECADES, CENTURIES."[9]

—STEPHANIE ZACHAREK, ELIANA DOCKTERMAN, AND HALEY SWEETLAND EDWARDS, *TIME* JOURNALISTS

Time magazine recognized those efforts with its Person of the Year title. Every year, *Time* gives the title to a person or group of people who have shaped national and international current events. In 2017, *Time* named the silence breakers as the Person of the Year. The article featured many women and some men who shared their experiences as survivors of sexual harassment and assault. The range of people was meant to show that sexual harassment and abuse affect people across categories. These categories include race, economic status, professional background, and age.

CURRENT REACH AND KEY DEBATES

Millions of people around the world have participated in the #MeToo movement. As silence

WHISPER NETWORKS

Before #MeToo, people used informal channels called whisper networks to warn one another of sexual harassers and abusers. Laura Palumbo is a director with the National Sexual Violence Resource Center (NSVRC). She explains that whisper networks allow people to share stories privately in their social circles when they do not have a safe avenue to share the information publicly. In Weinstein's case, many actors reported that Weinstein's behavior was an open secret among industry professionals because of the whisper network. For instance, actress Jessica Chastain says she heard stories about Weinstein early in her career. Actress Ashley Judd says she had been circulating her experience with Weinstein on the whisper network for years. Palumbo explains that whisper networks may help some people avoid predators. However, they are limited in how many people they reach and in their ability to end harassment and abuse.

breakers share their experiences, journalists continue to report stories about prominent figures in many fields, including politics, business, media, sports, education, and the arts. At the same time, people from all walks of life have evaluated the significance of #MeToo in their professional and personal interactions.

The movement also examines power structures that allow those violations to occur. Power stems from many sources, including professional roles, wealth, age, race/ethnicity, gender, and sexual orientation. As the #MeToo movement has evolved, all these factors have become parts of conversations about the movement's identity, development, goals, and future.

FROM THE
HEADLINES

BILL COSBY: BEFORE AND AFTER #METOO

In 2016, before the #MeToo hashtag went viral, Bill Cosby faced trial for sexual assault. Cosby is an actor and comedian. He is well known for starring on *The Cosby Show* in the 1980s and early 1990s. As of 2018, more than 60 women accused Cosby of sexual assault.[10] The allegations span several decades, reaching back to the 1960s. They include allegations from women who say they were drugged and raped. Some victims were under the age of 18.

One victim, Andrea Constand, filed a police report in 2005 after Cosby assaulted her. Cosby denied the allegations, claiming that Constand lied to get money from him. It took 11 years for the case to reach trial. Cosby's 2016 case ended in a mistrial, which means the jury could not agree on whether he was innocent or guilty.

Prosecutors retried the case in April 2018. The jury in the second trial found Cosby guilty of sexually assaulting Constand. Cosby's case was the first criminal trial against a major celebrity in the #MeToo era.

Bill Cosby, *right*, could spend up to 30 years in prison.

CHAPTER TWO

BEFORE
#METOO

The #MeToo movement questions the power dynamics and cultural norms that allow sexual harassment and abuse to occur. The majority of sexual harassment and abuse victims are women. Women have traditionally had limited power in legal, economic, political, and professional fields. For instance, in 1900, only 18 percent of working-age American women participated in the labor force.[1] That's because there were limited educational and employment opportunities available to them. Women's voices were not recognized in politics until 1920, when the Nineteenth Amendment extended the right to vote to women in the United States. Even after the passage of that amendment, many laws and social norms

In 1920, Kentucky governor Edwin P. Morrow signed the Nineteenth Amendment. Kentucky was the twenty-fourth state to approve it.

continued to disempower women. For instance, married women could not hold passports under their own names until the 1930s.

At the same time, social movements challenged these norms and systems of power. In the 1800s and early 1900s, women's groups organized for women's democratic rights in the political process. In the 1950s and 1960s, the civil rights movement led to the 1964 Civil Rights Act. Title VII of that act "prohibits employment discrimination based on race, color, religion, sex and national origin."[2] The act also created the Equal Employment Opportunity Commission (EEOC). This organization oversees and enforces federal laws about workplace discrimination. However, at the

Many people supported and fought for the Civil Rights Act.

time of their creation, neither Title VII nor the EEOC defined sexual harassment. Therefore, it was difficult for victims to seek legal options. During the 1970s, 1980s, and 1990s, women took steps to define the problem of sexual harassment and draw attention to it. Those steps paved the way for the #MeToo movement.

DEFINING THE PROBLEM

The term *sexual harassment* was popularized in 1975. It circulated among researchers at Cornell University and labor activists in response to an incident of workplace misconduct. The incident involved Carmita Wood, an administrative assistant in Cornell's Department of Nuclear Physics. In 1970, Wood's boss, the respected physicist Boyce McDaniel, began sexually harassing her. McDaniel was well known for his involvement with the Manhattan Project, a World War II (1939–1945) research effort that did crucial work on creating the first nuclear weapons.

McDaniel's actions toward Wood included jiggling his crotch when he was near her desk, brushing against her breasts, and groping her at professional social events. Wood experienced extreme stress and left her job.

She reached out to researchers in Cornell's Human Affairs Program (HAP) who were studying women and work.

Three instructors in HAP—Lin Farley, Susan Meyer, and Karen Sauvigné—wrote a letter to circulate to lawyers on Wood's behalf. They also began gathering insight from other women. For example, Farley raised the topic with students in her class and found that "each one of us had already quit or been fired from a job at least once because we had been made too uncomfortable by the behavior of men."[3] The students came from a range of backgrounds. They were rich, poor, black, and white.

HAP researchers noted that women were eager to break silence around these experiences, but no appropriate term existed for the problem. After brainstorming, members of HAP decided that *sexual harassment* conveyed the wide spectrum of inappropriate comments, looks, jokes, touches, and attacks women encountered.

The women of HAP began an organization called Working

"EVERY ONE OF US—THE WOMEN ON STAFF, CARMITA, THE STUDENTS—HAD HAD AN EXPERIENCE LIKE THIS AT SOME POINT, YOU KNOW? AND NONE OF US HAD EVER TOLD ANYONE BEFORE. IT WAS ONE OF THOSE CLICK, AHA! MOMENTS. A PROFOUND REVELATION."[4]

—LEADERS OF CORNELL'S HUMAN AFFAIRS PROGRAM IN THE 1970s

Women United. They reached out to employees at local factories, banks, and other companies to gain support and new members. They also contacted lawyers and members of the media and arranged what they called a speak out. The speak out was a public event to raise awareness and provide a place for people to share their experiences with sexual harassment. Almost 300 women attended the event.[5] It gained national attention later that year when it was mentioned in a *New York Times* story about sexual harassment.

The women who rallied behind Wood had started a discussion among themselves and in some national venues. Their actions were an early example of women's networks and labor organizations collaborating to break silence. It was also an example of the power and cultural dynamics that allow sexual harassment.

SETTING GUIDELINES AND SPEAKING OUT

Throughout the 1970s, 1980s, and 1990s, definitions of sexual harassment continued to evolve, as did efforts to prevent sexual harassment. In 1980, the EEOC established guidelines on sexual harassment for the first time. According to the guidelines, it was illegal to base employment decisions, such as promotions, on sexual favors. It was also illegal to create a hostile work environment through unwelcome sexual conduct.

The guidelines served as the basis in a landmark Supreme Court decision in 1986. In the case *Meritor Savings Bank v. Vinson*, Mechelle Vinson, an assistant branch manager at a bank, reported that her boss repeatedly harassed, assaulted, and raped her. The Supreme Court ruled that such behavior created a hostile work environment and was, therefore, sexual harassment under the EEOC's guidelines. It was the first case in which the Supreme Court concluded that sexual harassment was a form of employment discrimination under the law. Before this case, it was difficult to prove legally that harassment was a kind of discrimination rather than a personal matter.

Meritor Savings Bank v. Vinson was an important step against sexual harassment and assault. However, a scandal involving EEOC employees soon after the case demonstrated the difficulty in addressing harassment and assault. In 1991, lawyer Anita Hill gave a high-profile testimony about her former boss Clarence Thomas.

The testimony took place during a Senate hearing before Thomas was confirmed as a judge on the Supreme Court.

Hill had worked for Thomas at the Office of Civil Rights and at the EEOC. During that time, Hill said Thomas sexually harassed her by discussing graphic pornography, detailing his own sexual experiences, and repeatedly asking her on dates despite her refusals. Worried for her job and future, Hill did not report the incidents while she worked for Thomas. But when the FBI and Senate contacted her to conduct routine background checks on Thomas, Hill reported, "I felt that I had to tell the truth.

After Anita Hill accused Clarence Thomas of sexual harassment, she was subjected to victim blaming.

I could not keep silent."[6] By that time, Hill had obtained a new job as a law professor.

Hill faced challenging questions during a testimony before an all-male panel, as well as critical reactions and attacks on her character. These questions and reactions demonstrated victim blaming, shaming, discrediting, and denouncing. One senator asked her if she was speaking out because Thomas had hurt her feelings by refusing to start a relationship with her. Another senator faulted her for not putting a stop to Thomas's behavior. The senator asked, "How could you allow this kind of reprehensible conduct to go on right in the headquarters without doing something about it?"[7] Some dismissed the testimony as a he said/she said disagreement. A journalist famously labeled Hill as "a little bit nutty and a little bit slutty."[8]

Hill, who is black, also faced criticism for not supporting Thomas as he became only the second black Supreme Court justice in US history. Thomas denied Hill's statements and called the entire hearing a "high tech lynching."[9] Ultimately, the Senate confirmed Thomas as a Supreme Court justice by a vote of 52 in favor of Thomas and 48 against him.[10]

Though Hill faced harsh criticism, her situation drew attention to sexual harassment and motivated women's groups. In elections the following year, women won a record number of 24 seats in the House of Representatives. In the Senate, women also won a record of four new seats, which tripled the number of women in the Senate.[11] Among the newly elected women was Carol Moseley Braun, the first black woman to serve as a US senator.

While many factors contributed to the election results that year, one was Hill's testimony. The testimony was televised, so people were able to see and hear as Senate committee members, all white males, questioned Hill in a way that was sometimes belittling, hostile, and unsympathetic. The testimony left many

Clarence Thomas continued to serve on the Supreme Court into the year 2018.

people wondering who was representing women's voices in politics.

Other changes after Hill's testimony included a surge in the number of harassment claims reported to the EEOC. Those reports rose by 70 percent in the three months after her testimony.[12] Furthermore, President George H. W. Bush signed the Civil Rights Act of 1991. This act expanded the 1964 Civil Rights Act to include stronger protections against workplace harassment, including sexual harassment.

WHY NOW?

Previous social movements and the efforts of women such as Wood, Hill, and their supporters raised awareness about the cultural norms and power dynamics that allow sexual harassment and assault. Those efforts paved the way for #MeToo. But, given the long history of sexual harassment and abuse, people have considered why the tipping point for the movement only arrived in October 2017. Two of the most widely cited factors include the atmosphere around Donald Trump's election and presidency and the popularity of social media.

In October 2016, just one month before the presidential election, the *Washington Post* released a video from 2005 in which Trump made comments that objectified women. He mentioned kissing women aggressively and grabbing their genitals. Some people argued that those comments diminished the serious problem of sexual assault. Trump apologized for the comments on the video and acknowledged that he was embarrassed. However, in his statement of apology, Trump dismissed his language as "locker room banter."[13] The apology thus painted the comments as normal and acceptable in certain situations. He also turned attention away from his words by focusing on sexual harassment allegations against former president Bill Clinton, the husband of his political opponent, Hillary Clinton.

The video drew further attention to allegations of harassment and assault that had been made against

Trump for several years. It also prompted new allegations. Women claimed that Trump had forcibly kissed them, groped their breasts, reached up their skirts, and walked in on them as teenagers while they dressed and undressed for beauty pageants. The women's experiences occurred in both professional and social settings. Despite those allegations and the release of the video, Trump won the election in November 2016.

For victims and advocates, it was frustrating to see a president who joked about and allegedly perpetrated acts of harassment and assault. On January 21, 2017, the day after Trump's inauguration, millions of people gathered around the world at Women's March events to support women's rights. Rather than ending as a one-day event, the Women's March became a sustained effort to challenge powerful people who abuse others. The Women's March was an important precursor to the #MeToo movement. It helped establish a climate in which #MeToo could thrive.

The role of social media has also been essential to the spread of #MeToo. Social media offers a centralized, public space to anyone who wants to share their experiences.

MORE TO THE
STORY

PRESIDENTIAL SCANDALS AND THE 2016 ELECTION

Donald Trump was not the first president to be accused of inappropriate sexual conduct. Both before and after their elections, previous presidents have faced allegations of sexual misconduct, harassment, and scandal. The first official government involvement in a presidential sex scandal occurred while Bill Clinton was in office. In the late 1990s, investigators were looking into sexual harassment claims against Clinton when they discovered that Clinton had engaged in misconduct with an intern, Monica Lewinsky, in professional settings. Clinton was impeached in the House of Representatives. However, he was impeached for lying under oath and obstruction of justice in connection with the misconduct—not for the sexual misconduct itself. The Senate voted to clear Clinton, and he was not removed from office.

The issue of presidential misconduct received close attention in the 2016 election, not just because of the Trump allegations but also because Trump was running against Hillary Clinton. Hillary was the first woman to receive the presidential nomination from a major political party. Furthermore, much of Hillary's professional work as a lawyer and politician focused on women's and children's rights. However, she also remained married to someone who had engaged in inappropriate sexual conduct. Some people accused Hillary of protecting a sexual harasser. Other people argued that it was unfair to blame Hillary for her husband's actions.

The Women's March swept across the United States and became an international movement.

It also offers new options for silence breaking when more conventional avenues do not work. For example, Susan Fowler, an engineer for the transportation company Uber, first reported her experience with sexual harassment at Uber using the conventional methods. She told her managers and human resources staff at the company. However, management and human resources did not support her. The harassment continued. Fowler wrote a blog post about the experience. Once the post went viral, Uber CEO Travis Kalanick and several other executives resigned from the company over Fowler's claim and other scandals in the company.

Burke emphasizes how important social media is in spreading stories and helping people to see that they are not alone. She has noted, "The Internet is the great equalizer. The hashtag created a global community of support."[14] In this community, victims receive validation and empathy. They hear from others who have had similar experiences. In addition, they see harassers and abusers being held accountable. With that community and with the atmosphere created by the Women's March, silence breakers have been able to build on the long history of anti-harassment efforts to create the #MeToo movement.

NAMING NAMES ON SOCIAL MEDIA

There are many debates in the #MeToo movement regarding how much attention to give to accused perpetrators. One key debate deals with naming harassers and abusers on social media. Some people oppose naming names because it places the spotlight on the accused when people should focus on helping victims and broadening discussions about the problem. Author Anne Ursu took this position in an essay about sexual harassment in children's book publishing. In the essay, Ursu wrote, "Once names are involved people start defending the harassers and accusing the harassed . . . it stops the conversation before it starts."[15] On the other hand, some people believe that naming names is an important part of breaking silence and that public accountability is crucial.

FROM THE HEADLINES

REFUSING THE #METOO LABEL

Stormy Daniels, an adult film actress whose real name is Stephanie Clifford, made headlines for stating she had a sexual encounter with President Trump while he was married. She says the encounter occurred in 2006, before Trump was elected president. Daniels signed a nondisclosure agreement in 2016. As part of the agreement, Trump's lawyer Michael Cohen paid her $130,000 not to speak about the encounter.[16] Trump's legal team said the agreement occurred at that time to avoid bad publicity before the election.

Daniels rejects the label of victim. She says that her encounter with Trump does not fall within the #MeToo movement. She argues that labeling her experience as such diminishes the stories of real victims. Journalists who agree with Daniels believe that efforts to include her story in the #MeToo movement are overreaching and could lead to a slippery slope. They claim, as Daniels does, that the slippery slope unfairly presents all women as passive victims rather than as individuals with a choice.

Stormy Daniels came forward with her story in early 2018.

34

#METOO IN THE
WORKPLACE

The Weinstein news story that prompted the viral hashtag #MeToo in October 2017 was a story related to work. Actresses and industry professionals went to meetings with Weinstein to discuss business. Instead of participating in a meeting, they found themselves subjected to sexual harassment and assault. Many of the efforts in the 1970s, 1980s, and 1990s, before #MeToo, also focused on sexual harassment and assault at work. Rebecca Traister, a writer who covers women's rights issues, argues that workplace sexual harassment and assault devalues people by treating them as sex objects rather than skilled professionals.

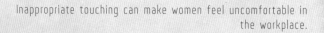

Inappropriate touching can make women feel uncomfortable in the workplace.

Not only is workplace sexual misconduct devaluing; it also threatens people's livelihoods. When harassment and abuse occur at work, victims often express feelings of fear and powerlessness because of the effects that speaking out may have on their jobs, such as getting fired. This potential financial impact has led activists to use strong wording and label workplace harassment as "a type of 'economic rape.'"[1] Even in less extreme cases, employees may worry they will be seen as difficult to get along with if they make a report and will receive fewer opportunities for advancement.

Work-related stories from the #MeToo movement have spanned industries including media, arts, sports, food service, technology, education, medicine, agriculture, hospitality, and domestic work. Researchers agree that workplace sexual misconduct has been and continues to be a widespread problem. Polls from late 2017 and early 2018 reported that almost one-half of women have experienced workplace sexual harassment.[2] About

14 percent of men have experienced workplace sexual harassment as well.[4] Given these statistics and the significance of workplace harassment in the #MeToo movement, some people have said that #MeToo is a workers' rights movement.

WHAT CONSTITUTES SEXUAL HARASSMENT AT WORK

Workplace sexual harassment can be hard to define and can take many forms. The legal definition currently used by the EEOC includes "unwelcome sexual advances, requests for sexual favors, and other verbal or physical harassment of a sexual nature."[5] Harassment can also involve broadly offensive remarks such as inappropriate observations about women. Perpetrators of workplace sexual misconduct can be victims' supervisors. But they

WORKPLACE HARASSMENT IN OTHER COUNTRIES

By the end of October 2017, social media users in 85 countries had participated in the #MeToo movement.[6] Those users revealed workplace sexual misconduct as a global problem. Addressing the problem is difficult in countries that do not have specific laws against workplace harassment. Research by the WORLD Policy Analysis Center shows that, as of 2017, 68 countries had no laws specifically prohibiting workplace sexual harassment.[7] Those countries are spread throughout the world, but there are particularly high concentrations in Africa, Asia, and the Middle East. Additionally, some countries such as Ethiopia, China, and India do not include harassment against men in their workplace laws.

"A RAPIST QUITE OFTEN USES A GUN OR A KNIFE—SOMETIMES ONLY BRUTE STRENGTH. A MALE BOSS OR SUPERVISOR USES HIS ECONOMIC POWER TO HIRE AND FIRE AS HIS WEAPON."[8]

—CARMITA WOOD, ANTI-HARASSMENT ACTIVIST

can also be other people in a professional setting, including coworkers, clients, and customers.

Some examples from the #MeToo movement demonstrate the many forms that harassment may take. This range is apparent in both celebrity and noncelebrity experiences. In the case of longtime journalist Charlie Rose, silence breakers reported that he made lewd phone calls, grabbed victims, and walked around naked in front of them. All of Rose's accusers were fellow journalists or his assistants.

In the case of acclaimed chef and TV personality Mario Batali, silence breakers noted his decades-long pattern of inappropriate groping, bullying, intimidation, and offensive comments. Some comments included him asking about his employees' underwear. In the case of James Levine, a famous conductor, silence breakers' stories revealed controlling and abusive treatment of his students. Levine's behavior included pressuring musicians to engage in sex acts with him and with their colleagues. In her

#MeToo story, a doctor remembered a patient who forcibly kissed her in her own office. A prison guard disclosed her experience with a staff sergeant who scheduled shifts so that she would be alone and he could rape her.

Workplace sexual harassment and abuse can be especially hard for employees working in low-wage or customer-service jobs. For example, waitstaff have been among the #MeToo voices that shed light on out-of-control harassment and abuse for people in these professions. Waitstaff often earn less than minimum wage and depend on customer tips. As a result, they often feel pressured to tolerate verbal and physical harassment or risk losing pay. Lita Farquhar, a waitress from New Orleans, Louisiana, explained, "It's really hard when a customer sexually

Some restaurants require waitresses to wear revealing clothing to help their business.

harasses you, because as a server, I make $2.13 an hour and I really rely on tips."[9]

Farquhar also reported receiving little support from management when harassment and abuse occurred. Management may even encourage waitstaff to accept harassment and flirt with customers to boost business. The #MeToo movement has also drawn attention to the widespread sexual misconduct that occurs in other jobs that are low wage, overlooked, and isolated, such as farmwork, domestic work, janitorial work, and hotel housekeeping.

THE CAUSES AND EFFECTS OF SEXUAL HARASSMENT AT WORK

Stories from the #MeToo movement reveal that many factors contribute to workplace harassment and abuse. People are especially vulnerable to harassment and abuse when they are in positions of economic dependence or in positions with little or no authority. Women and minorities have historically faced unequal representation in leadership roles and economic challenges such as pay gaps. Those groups are also at higher risk for sexual harassment and abuse.

Research also indicates that many professions still perpetuate cultures that allow for sexual misconduct. This problem is especially clear in traditionally male-dominated professions such as medicine, engineering, and law enforcement. It is also evident in professions with strict hierarchies of authority, such as the military. In certain professional environments, silence breakers mention feeling as though they are in a "boys' club," where dealing with harassment and abuse within the hierarchy has always been and feels like it might always be a standard part of the job.[11]

The effects of workplace sexual misconduct may be psychological, physical, and economic. People who experience workplace sexual harassment might miss work due to their symptoms or because they want to avoid harassment. Victims might also be less productive as they struggle with symptoms, distractions, and efforts to avoid their harassers. Victims might leave their jobs even if that means starting over at a new job with lower pay or lower seniority. For example, a data scientist recalls leaving her job in academia for a lower-paying job in the nonprofit sector to escape the culture of abuse in her former industry. Sociology researchers have found that women who experience sexual harassment are six and one-half times more likely to leave their jobs than women who do not experience harassment.[12] For employees with limited financial resources, these effects can mean further economic struggles.

TIME'S UP ON WORKPLACE HARASSMENT

In addition to calling attention to widespread workplace sexual harassment and abuse,

NEW LAWS TO CHANGE WORKPLACE CULTURE

Lawmakers have proposed legislative initiatives to end workplace practices that allow sexual misconduct. For instance, in December 2017, Senators Kirsten Gillibrand, a Democrat from New York, and Lindsey Graham, a Republican from South Carolina, introduced the Ending the Forced Arbitration of Sexual Harassment Act. The act's goal is to eliminate forced arbitration clauses in employee contracts. Forced arbitration clauses require employees to address harassment within a system established by their employer. Under those clauses, the employee cannot discuss the case outside of that system or take the case before a jury trial. Jury trials are often fairer to the victim. Arbitration clauses usually protect perpetrators and employers. Approximately 60 million Americans have forced arbitration clauses in their contracts.[13] The act notes that abolishing those clauses would help bring down workplace cultures that silence victims and enable harassment.

Tina Tchen, *left*, helped create the Time's Up Legal Defense Fund.

the #MeToo movement aims to address issues that create

hostile environments and power disparities in professional

environments. An offshoot of the #MeToo movement

called the Time's Up Legal Defense Fund targets those

objectives. It promotes equality in the workplace, in

pay, and in leadership positions. Time's Up also seeks to

improve laws, employment agreements, and corporate

policies. Furthermore, it offers financial assistance to help

with the high costs of filing lawsuits against harassers.

Time's Up has raised millions of dollars, and workers from

many industries have reached out for assistance.

CHAPTER FOUR

THE MOVEMENT
OUTSIDE OF
WORK

T he #MeToo movement has prompted people to discuss sexual harassment and abuse in relationships. It's also sparked conversations about street harassment and other sexual misconduct in public spaces. Sexual misconduct in friendships, families, marriages, partnerships, and dating relationships is underreported. However, reports available show that sexual abuse by family members is a significant problem.

The US Department of Justice and experts at the Crimes Against Children Research Center report

Abusive relationships can take a heavy toll on people's emotional and physical health.

that a family member is the perpetrator in many child sexual abuse cases. Intimate partner sexual violence, which includes sexual violence in marriages and dating relationships, is also a significant problem. A 2015 Centers for Disease Control and Prevention (CDC) survey found that about 18 percent of women and 8 percent of men had suffered a form of intimate partner sexual violence during their lifetimes.[1]

Breaking silence on harassment and abuse in families and relationships can be especially difficult. The victim may care about or love the abuser and hesitate to report the abuse. The victim may also worry about causing pain or trouble within families and friendships by disclosing sexual misconduct. Feelings of fear, guilt, and shame can also silence a victim.

Furthermore, when abuse or harassment occurs in close relationships, it can be difficult for others to believe the reports. For example, one family member may be reluctant to accept accusations against another family member. In addition, victims may be financially dependent on their abusers. This is often the case when the victim is a minor or when the victim does not work or earns less than an abusive partner. Victims may share their home with their abusers. When emotional and money concerns combine, it can be very difficult for survivors to come forward.

Some advocates say that the #MeToo movement must do more to eliminate barriers to reporting abuse within families and intimate partnerships. These barriers include the belief that harassment and abuse cannot occur in families, friendships, or intimate partnerships.

Keysha Lleras, a survivor of intimate partner violence, says there is a stigma around harassment and abuse in families and intimate partnerships that will only "be fixed if we continue to tell our stories."[2] Advocates also call for a destigmatizing discussion of incest, which remains a taboo

MARITAL RAPE

Laws acknowledging marital rape as a crime are relatively new. The first state to make marital rape a crime was Nebraska in 1976. By 1993, all states had criminalized marital rape. Before this time, there was a marital rape exemption. This prevented rape charges from being filed if the people involved were married. Even with criminal laws in place, several states make it harder to prosecute marital rape than other rapes. State laws include narrower definitions of marital rape, more lenient penalties for perpetrators, and harder reporting procedures for victims. For example, in Ohio, marital rape is illegal only if there is use of force or threat rather than solely a lack of consent. In South Carolina, a victim has only 30 days to report marital rape, but there is no statute of limitations for other crimes of sexual violence in this state. A statute of limitations requires legal action to begin within a set time frame after an alleged crime.

topic that receives little attention. The Rape, Abuse, and Incest National Network reports evidence that the #MeToo movement has made some progress in encouraging more victims to break their silence.

PUBLIC SPACES AND STREET HARASSMENT

Some silence breakers have also pointed out the prevalence of street harassment. Even though street harassment is very common, there is no single, universal definition of the term. The Advocates for Human Rights, a nonprofit organization, uses a broad definition: "Street harassment is verbal, physical, or psychological harm done to women in public spaces."[3] Stop Street Harassment, another nonprofit organization, adds that although street

Stares from men on the street can make many women feel uncomfortable.

harassment is more commonly experienced by women, it may affect men as well. Street harassment is a form of sexual harassment because it targets people based on their gender and sexual identity. Street harassment happens commonly on public transportation. Examples of street harassment range from whistling, honking, making vulgar gestures or sexist comments, and catcalling to groping, stalking, and assault.

Street harassment is often trivialized and overlooked because it happens so frequently. A 2014 national survey of 2,000 adults found that 65 percent of women and 25 percent of men had experienced street harassment at some point in their lives.[4] Street harassment is so common that many people view it as a normal occurrence that they simply have to put up with. Some people also view street harassment as an innocent expression of free speech.

Some silence breakers seek to challenge the normalization and acceptance of street harassment. The #MeToo movement identifies street harassment as a symptom of long-standing social and cultural traditions that objectify and sexualize people—especially women and minorities. #MeToo advocates claim that street harassment is a reminder that for much of history, women and minorities did not have the same rights, freedoms, and protections as white men. Women and minorities also did not have equal access to public spaces. When women and minorities entered those spaces, there was a misconception that their bodies were available for public viewing and commentary.

The #MeToo movement calls attention to those historical norms and to contemporary attitudes that enable street harassment. Silence breakers point out that street harassment has negative effects. For example, street harassment disempowers the people it targets because it involves a one-way interaction. The harasser controls the situation. The victim must either endure the harassment or prolong the experience by confronting the harasser. The victim has no way of knowing whether a confrontation will escalate the harassment. The victim also doesn't know whether ignoring the harassment will provoke more aggressive behavior as the harasser tries to get a response.

"THE GUY MAY NOT UNDERSTAND IT'S WRONG. HE MAY THINK HE'S GIVING A COMPLIMENT."[5]

—GEORGE GARRISON, HIGH SCHOOL STUDENT INVOLVED IN AN ANTI-HARASSMENT PROGRAM

Furthermore, the burden of avoiding harassment usually falls on the victim. People who have experienced street harassment report changing their attire, transportation choices, and routines to avoid harassment. For example, a person who has experienced street harassment while out jogging may feel compelled to switch habits and pay for a gym membership rather than endure the harassment she faces on the street.

DEBATES SURROUNDING #METOO OUTSIDE OF WORK

Among the biggest debates surrounding the #MeToo movement are those that raise questions about gray areas in sexual misconduct outside of work. The gray area debate has come up in consideration of personal relationships as well as in discussions of street harassment.

Recent viral stories have demonstrated concerns about ambiguity in personal

"FOR ME, IT HAS ALWAYS BEEN MORE THAN AN ANNOYANCE. IT'S SHAPED MY EXPERIENCE IN PUBLIC SPACE. IT'S AFFECTED MY CONFIDENCE AND COMFORT WALKING DOWN THE STREET. IT'S SILENCED ME—I'VE NEVER FELT COMFORTABLE RESPONDING TO CATCALLS, AS MUCH AS I'D LIKE TO TELL THESE MEN OFF."[6]

—SOPHIE SANDBERG, COLLEGE STUDENT

relationships. For example, the short story "Cat Person" by Kristen Roupenian presented a fictional account of a 20-year-old female college student, Margot, who began a relationship with Robert—a man in his thirties. The relationship progressed to an uncomfortable sexual encounter. The encounter was not a violent assault or rape, but it left Margot feeling pressured, confused, unhappy, and no longer interested in seeing Robert. However, Robert continued to message Margot. He showed up at a bar he knew Margot frequented. Then, he sent her a text insulting her after seeing her at the bar with a male friend. Though fictional, the story resonated with many people.

Some people who are accused of harassment say they didn't realize their actions were inappropriate.

The story raised questions about consent, approaches to exiting uncomfortable situations, sexual expectations in dating culture, and feelings of guilt, shame, and confusion. Many people have argued that these are important questions to discuss as part of the #MeToo movement. Others believe "Cat Person" and real-life experiences similar to it fall outside the scope of #MeToo. From this point of view, those experiences are misunderstandings, miscommunications, or minor offenses. Some people worry that such stories may confuse the movement and undermine attention that should be given to serious, predatory harassment and violence. This same concern comes up in regard to street harassment, especially when the harassment is perceived by some people as relatively minor—such as whistles, honks, or catcalls. Critics point out that there is potential harm in lumping off-color comments and minor incidents within the same movement as predatory harassment and violent assaults.

MINORS IN THE
MOVEMENT

On October 18, 2017, Olympic gymnast McKayla Maroney emerged as a silence breaker when she posted her #MeToo story on Twitter. Maroney identified her sexual abuser as her doctor Larry Nassar. Nassar worked for the US Women's Gymnastics Team, the Olympic Team, Michigan State University (MSU), and several gymnastic facilities. Maroney says that Nassar took advantage of his position as a trusted authority figure and a medical professional. Because of his role as a physician, young patients believed that Nassar's actions, which included fondling their genitals and using his bare fingers to penetrate their vaginas and rectums, were routine medical treatments for muscle pain and athletic injuries. Nassar also groped girls'

Rachael Denhollander, a former gymnast, was the first woman to accuse Nassar of sexual abuse.

breasts, exposed himself, and masturbated in front of them. Maroney challenged Nassar's misuse of power. She wrote, "This is happening everywhere. Wherever there is a position of power, there seems to be potential for abuse."[1]

Maroney's statement was not the first or only such account related to Nassar. When Maroney posted her message, Nassar was already facing charges of child pornography and sexual assault. However, Maroney was the most high-profile gymnast to address her experience publicly up to that point. By early 2018, more than 200 survivors had shared their experiences, and Nassar was sentenced to 60 years in prison for child pornography charges and up to 300 years in prison for child sexual abuse.[2]

Survivors who broke their silence on Nassar revealed the widespread and systemic nature of sexual harassment and abuse. They mentioned the coaches and other adults, gymnastics organizations, medical groups, educational programs, and law enforcement officers that could have stopped Nassar but failed to do so. In many cases of harassment and abuse exposed by the #MeToo movement, a system of institutions and individuals ignore, enable,

Kaylee Lorincz was one of more than 100 women to address Nassar in court.

or protect the abusers. The effect of those systems is especially evident when victims are minors. Nassar's case is one example.

WHY IT IS DIFFICULT FOR MINORS TO BREAK SILENCE

Research gathered by the CDC estimates that about one in four girls and one in six boys are sexually abused before they turn 18 years old.[3] However, government organizations believe the rates are actually higher than the research reports.

In most cases of child sex abuse, the perpetrator is someone the child knows. According to research by the US Department of Justice and experts at the Crimes Against Children Research Center, the perpetrator in about one-third of child sexual abuse cases is a family member. In 59 percent of cases, the perpetrator is an acquaintance other than a family member. In only 7 percent of cases is the perpetrator a stranger.[4]

Because children often know the perpetrator, sexual abuse commonly goes unreported. Children may want to protect the abuser, or they may fear the abuser. Power dynamics between children and adults also prevent minors from breaking their silence. Those dynamics encourage children to trust adults and discourage adults from believing children. A common misconception is that children make up false accusations that they later take back.

THE EFFECT OF CHILDHOOD SEX ABUSE

Research connects childhood sexual harassment and abuse to emotional, behavioral, psychological, and physical problems. Silence breakers in the Nassar case spoke of their alcohol dependence and addiction, anorexia, suicidal thoughts, nightmares, anxiety, depression, breakdowns, and severe stomach pain. Childhood sexual abuse often continues to affect people into adulthood.

MORE TO THE
STORY

#METOOK12

The nonprofit organization Stop Sexual Harassment in Schools started the #MeTooK12 campaign to accompany the larger #MeToo movement. The aim of #MeTooK12 is to confront the problem of sexual misconduct in schools. Peer sexual harassment and bullying are common problems, and peer sexual assault occurs too. A 2014 study found that about 68 percent of girls and 55 percent of boys reported at least one experience of sexual harassment in high school.[5] However, students, schools, and school districts do not often report the problem. Between 2013 and 2014, the majority of schools teaching grades 7–12 reported no incidents of sexual harassment. Furthermore, attention from media and lawmakers often focuses on sexual misconduct in higher education rather than in elementary, middle, and high schools.

The #MeTooK12 movement points out that addressing sexual harassment early can help change the culture that enables sexual misconduct later on in colleges, workplaces, and public spaces. Some states have already broadened their sexual health education curricula to include these topics. For example, California's Healthy Youth Act requires curricula that discuss issues such as consent, victim blaming, and street harassment. However, more than one-half of states do not require topics such as consent to be covered. While advocates see #MeTooK12 as a positive extension of the #MeToo movement, others argue that these topics are too sensitive for school settings. Instead, they note, parents and caretakers should be responsible for educating minors on topics of sexual harassment and violence.

Children's developing ability to understand, process, and communicate abuse also makes reporting difficult. Minors may not always understand what sexual abuse is or that abuse has occurred. In addition, they may not have the same communication skills as adults to report their abuse. Examples of the struggle to understand and disclose abuse occurred in Nassar's case. When young athletes felt confused about their treatment, they would sometimes confide in one another. One silence breaker remembers, "We all talked about how it was uncomfortable and we really didn't like it and it didn't help, but it happened to all of us, so we thought it was normal."[6] Some of these survivors did not realize until they were older, with more education and experience, that Nassar's actions were abusive.

THE SYSTEMS THAT IGNORE AND ENABLE ABUSE

People began making reports against Nassar in the mid-1990s. For instance, in 1997, a parent brought concerns about abuse to John Geddert, the owner of Twistars Gymnastics Club. Around the same time, two student-athletes at MSU disclosed their abusive experiences with Nassar to athletic staff. Those reports did not result in action. Law enforcement was not notified, and Nassar was not removed from patient care. Law enforcement was notified in 2004 when a victim contacted a local police department in Michigan to report abuse. Police interviewed the girl and Nassar, but police believed Nassar's explanation about medical technique over the girl's account.

In 2014, MSU conducted a Title IX investigation into student Amanda Thomashow's disclosure about Nassar. Title IX is a federal law meant to protect people in education programs from sex discrimination, which

Some gymnasts who were abused by Nassar also placed blame on John Geddert for not protecting them.

MINORS, CLASS, AND SEXUAL VIOLENCE

While sexual harassment and abuse affect people at all income levels, there is a connection between poverty and sexual violence. People who live in poverty are more vulnerable to sexual violence than people with higher socioeconomic status. Minors are among those most disproportionately affected by sexual violence and poverty. Several factors increase the risk of sexual violence for poor children. These include unsafe neighborhoods, unstable family units, and lack of affordable childcare options, which may lead parents to leave children unattended or with caretakers who are not properly qualified. Children who depend on the foster system for care are ten times more likely to experience sexual abuse than children who live with both biological parents.[7]

includes harassment and abuse. The MSU investigator told Thomashow they did not find any evidence of misconduct. However, a private, internal report included suspicions about Nassar's behavior. But no legal action came against Nassar at that time.

In 2015, officials at USA Gymnastics and the US Olympic Committee learned of accusations against Nassar. Officials also learned about an FBI investigation into the accusations. The FBI investigation and responses from USA Gymnastics and the US Olympic Committee have received criticism for being too slow. None of those organizations stepped in to prevent Nassar from seeing and abusing patients at MSU. He continued his work there until late in 2016 when he was fired and indicted on charges. Throughout this span of about two decades, other athletes told parents, coaches, trainers, and medical staff about Nassar's abuse. Furthermore, one survivor, Kyle Stephens,

whose parents were friends with Nassar, reported Nassar to Child Protective Services, to counselors, and to medical licensing bodies, but action was slow.

In the fallout of the Nassar case, authority figures at many institutions lost their jobs. Among them were several officials from MSU, including the university's president, athletic director, gymnastics coach, school doctor, vice president for legal affairs, and dean of the College of Osteopathic Medicine. At USA Gymnastics, the entire board of directors resigned under pressure. The CEOs of USA Gymnastics and the US Olympic Committee also resigned under pressure. Many of these officials faced lawsuits, and some faced criminal charges.

THE EFFECT OF #METOO FOR MINORS

Silence breakers in the Nassar case have demonstrated the effect #MeToo can have on exposing the systemic problems that enable abuse of minors. Furthermore, survivors in this case show the importance of solidarity and sharing stories. Stephens was able to identify her experience as abuse only after seeing news stories about another abuse case and talking with a friend who had also been molested. Jamie Dantzscher, an Olympic gymnast, says she also only came to terms with her abuse after speaking with a friend who had been abused by a coach. Rachael Denhollander, a former gymnast, began to share her story after reading an article about another case of abuse. She then emailed a newspaper with her experience. Jacob Moore, the first male victim to speak out

Jamie Dantzscher confronted Nassar in court.

against Nassar, came forward after hearing his sister break her silence.

Maroney posted her tweet after being inspired by others in the #MeToo movement. Many survivors in the Nassar case originally wanted to be anonymous or did not want to speak in public at Nassar's sentencing hearing. However, when they witnessed dozens of other people voicing their stories, they felt empowered as part of a group. Victim impact statements at Nassar's sentencing included stories from survivors who are now adults as well as stories from survivors who are still minors.

"ONE OF THE MOST INCREDIBLE THINGS IS TO SEE THE PROSECUTOR WALK UP AND SAY, 'OUR NEXT VICTIM IS GOING TO BE ANONYMOUS, PLEASE TURN OFF THE CAMERAS' AND THEN THE PERSON GETS UP IN THE COURTROOM AND SAYS, 'YOU KNOW, I'VE CHANGED MY MIND. I'M GOING TO SPEAK NOW.'"[9]

—KYLE STEPHENS, SEXUAL ASSAULT ADVOCATE AND SURVIVOR

THE #METOO MOVEMENT AND RACE

Women of color have been pioneers in fighting sexual harassment throughout the 1900s and in founding the #MeToo movement. At the same time, many communities of color continue to experience sexual harassment and violence at higher rates than white communities, often without receiving the same level of visibility and support as survivors within the white community. As a result, the #MeToo movement has faced criticism for focusing on white celebrities without acknowledging the contributions of

Women of all races and ethnicities have participated in the #MeToo movement.

BLACK FEMALE VOTERS

The #MeToo movement received attention in the December 2017 Alabama election. During the campaign, several women accused the Republican candidate Roy Moore of sexual harassment and assault. Moore's opponent, Democrat Doug Jones, won the election. Alabama is traditionally a Republican state. A Democrat had not won a Senate election in Alabama in the previous 25 years.

Exit polls showed that the strongest critics of Moore were black women. Ninety-eight percent of black female voters voted against Moore in favor of Jones. Meanwhile, only 34 percent of white women voted for Jones.[1] This percentage was noteworthy because white women in Alabama typically support Republican candidates at much higher percentages. However, it remained clear that black women were strongest in opposition to Moore. Several issues affected the election. Many of those issues were of particular concern to black women. These included affordable health care and rising rates of incarceration among black women. However, #MeToo also became a central issue. Commentators have observed that black women's efforts in campaigning and voting against Moore demonstrate their leadership in social movements, which often has an impact but goes unrecognized.

people of color or addressing the obstacles victims of color encounter.

People of color face many of the same challenges that white survivors face in their experience with abuse and harassment and their attempts to report it. There are feelings of guilt, shame, and confusion; fear of professional damage; and worries about economic impact. However, people of color often confront additional difficulties in breaking their silence. Those difficulties may vary depending on whether the perpetrator is of the same race as the victim or of a different race. People of color may also face cultural pressure to remain silent, pressure that can cause worry about retribution or isolation within their communities if they break silence.

CULTURAL STEREOTYPES THAT CONTRIBUTE TO SILENCE

Stereotypes and historical prejudices have contributed to sexualization and objectification of people of color. When sharing her #MeToo experiences, Zahira Kelly-Cabrera, an artist who is Afro-Dominican, notes, "Certain bodies are just not as protected as others and that's a historical thing."[2] She traces the problem to the history of racial inequality in the United States, which includes black slavery and violent treatment of Native Americans. In the 1600s through the 1800s, enslaved people were considered property. This allowed white men to sexually abuse and rape slaves without consequences. Some slaveholders forced slaves to have sex with one another in order to enslave any children who were born. In other cases, slaveholders raped enslaved women for the same purpose.

Predominant white society also viewed Native Americans as inferior, impure, and unworthy of respect.

As was the case with black slaves, laws did not protect Native Americans from rape. Sexual abuse was also used as a real and a symbolic method to apply dominance and control over Native Americans. As white populations settled the country, Native Americans faced high rates of sexual abuse. Though laws now protect Native American communities, high rates of abuse still affect Native Americans. The Department of Justice reports that "American Indians are 2.5 times more likely to experience sexual assault compared to all other races."[3] Overall, about 56 percent of Native American women experience sexual violence.[4]

THE STRUGGLE TO BREAK SILENCE WITHIN COMMUNITIES OF COLOR

Silence breakers from communities of color have noted that sharing #MeToo stories has different implications depending on whether the perpetrator is of the same race as the victim or of a different race. When the perpetrator is of the same race as the victim, people of color often feel pressured into silence. They feel that reporting their

There are high rates of domestic violence in Native American communities, but some people are able to escape those situations.

harassment and abuse may lead to further stereotyping of their race and undo progress.

Mary Annette Pember, a Native American journalist and photographer, has written about this difficulty within the Native American community. One woman, who chose to remain anonymous in Pember's article, noted, "Indian Country is so marginalized that when we see someone do well and receive recognition, we don't want to participate in anything that would take them down." The woman had been harassed by a Native American man who was prominent in his professional field. The man was well recognized for his contributions both within and outside of the Native American community. "I wrestled with my importance versus his," the woman said.[5] Silence breakers speaking out against Sherman Alexie, an honored writer known for bringing attention to the Native American community through literature, voiced similar concerns.

Silence breakers may fear that their stories will be viewed as betrayals, which could lead to isolation and retribution. The woman in Pember's story explained, "Most Native communities are small and tightly knit. Publicly accusing a man in authority of sexual harassment or assault can open up one's entire family for retribution. Housing, employment, access to services, and even enrollment in the tribe might be jeopardized."[6]

Farah Tanis is a sexual assault survivor who founded Black Women's Blueprint—a nonprofit that aims to empower black women. She describes similar obstacles in close-knit black communities where groups such as families and churches are intertwined. Revealing abuse within those communities can feel like a betrayal at many levels. It can also disturb the dynamics at the heart of the community. Family concerns also run deep in traditional Hispanic communities, says Neusa Gaytan, who works with Mujeres Latinas en Acción, an organization that advocates for the Latina community.

In 2018, members of Black Women's Blueprint created a mural to show their support for black women who have been sexually assaulted.

Furthermore, survivors may struggle to break silence because they distrust and fear the systems that are supposed to help them. Racism in law enforcement, social service agencies, and health care can make it difficult for survivors to file reports. For example, a black victim might be reluctant to report an abuser from her community out of fear that he might then become the victim of police brutality. If people of color choose to disclose to law enforcement officers, social service workers, or health-care providers, they face high rates of disbelief and victim blaming based on stereotypes.

#MOSQUEMETOO

Author and activist Mona Eltahawy started the hashtag #MosqueMeToo in response to stories of sexual misconduct circulating among Muslim women on social media. One story, written by a Pakistani woman named Sabica Khan, focused on an experience during hajj. Hajj is a pilgrimage to Mecca, Saudi Arabia, required of all Muslims who are healthy enough and financially able to travel. Khan described being groped as she performed tawaf—a ritual of walking seven circles around the sanctuary in the Great Mosque. Khan said she first thought the groping was an accident because the Great Mosque is very crowded during hajj. When it happened more than once, she knew it was intentional. Hundreds of other people shared similar experiences. These silence breakers mention the taboo of sexual misconduct in places of worship. They also discuss fears that sharing experiences will result in Islamophobic reactions, perpetuate stereotypes, or lead to backlash and restrictions for Muslim women. However, advocates emphasize that such stories are important in the effort to eliminate gender-based violence in Muslim communities.

ADVOCATING FOR CHANGE

When victims in communities of color have made efforts to break silence, they have frequently encountered challenges in gaining widespread support for change and justice. Women of color point out that efforts to condemn musician R. Kelly for predatory sexual behavior toward black girls and women have not seen the same results as efforts to condemn Weinstein.

One silence breaker, Jerhonda Pace, disclosed that R. Kelly abused her in 2009. She has been trying to raise awareness and find justice since the summer of 2017 for herself and other victims. When she saw the quick spread of #MeToo after the Weinstein article, Pace remembers, "I was livid, because when their stories came out, they received so much attention. It was just crazy, and I was like, 'What about R. Kelly's victims? What about us?' Nothing happened for us."[7]

The rapid support for a movement popularized through rich, white, celebrity culture is a reminder for people of color that silence is harder to break for those who are marginalized. Burke, too, worries that the central message of her movement—bringing change to black and brown communities—may be lost in the trending spotlight and in the attention given to high-profile men and women.

Some people have chosen not to participate in the current #MeToo movement because they believe it has not done enough to acknowledge previous efforts by people of color and continued attacks on marginalized communities. However, others, including Burke, believe that white, wealthy, celebrity attention to the #MeToo movement and the subsequent Time's Up campaign can help draw awareness to marginalized people who have suffered sexual abuse and harassment.

CHAPTER SEVEN

GENDER AND
SEXUAL
ORIENTATION

Alyssa Milano's viral October 2017 tweet called on "all the women" who had experienced sexual harassment to spread the post.[1] The phrasing in the tweet brought attention to the role of gender in the #MeToo movement. Similarly, the *Time* cover photo that names the silence breakers as the Person of the Year features only women. The accompanying article includes some stories and photographs of men, but the dominant photograph focuses on women. Some people contend that #MeToo is fundamentally about exposing and ending long-standing misogyny

Actor Terry Crews shared his #MeToo story after the Weinstein scandal broke. Crews said he was sexually assaulted by a Hollywood executive in 2016.

FEMALE PERPETRATORS

In more than 90 percent of rape and sexual violence cases involving female victims, the perpetrator is male. In more than 90 percent of rape cases involving a male victim, the perpetrator is also male.[2] However, in other types of sexual violence and harassment involving male victims, the perpetrator is often female. But female perpetrators do not receive much attention. Just as there are stereotypes that men and boys cannot be victims, there are stereotypes that women and girls cannot be perpetrators of sexual harassment or violence. Those stereotypes present women and girls as always being nurturing and submissive. Some researchers argue that stereotypes of both men and women harm efforts to address harassment and abuse.

in society. Misogyny tolerates, enables, and encourages sexual harassment and violence by men against women. This point of view does not dismiss other forms of oppression and misuses of power. However, it argues that those issues should be addressed in a different forum.

Some people have critiqued this view as too narrow. Instead, they argue #MeToo should bring awareness to people of all genders and sexual orientations who have experienced sexual misconduct and want to share their stories. This view claims that doing so will help to reveal the many dynamics in society that allow sexual abuse and harassment. It will also highlight the voices of people often overlooked in conversations about sexual harassment and abuse. Those include men and members of the LGBTQ community.

Advocates note that including a range of voices strengthens the movement.

MEN AND #METOO

The majority of sexual harassment and violence victims are female. However, men and boys also experience sexual harassment and abuse. A 2013 survey of 40,000 households nationwide reported that men were the victims in 38 percent of rapes and sexual assaults.[3] A poll released by Marketplace-Edison in 2018 found that one in seven men said they had experienced sexual harassment at work.[4] Researchers believe sexual harassment and assault against male victims is actually much higher than these reports show because cases often go unreported.

Many groups face barriers to disclosing abuse and harassment. For men and boys, those barriers include society's view of masculinity. Expectations about masculinity suggest that men are supposed to enjoy and be proud of all sexual experiences. Traditional concepts of masculinity also imply that men and boys should be strong and active. These concepts promote the myth that men and boys should be able to defend themselves from an assault.

Because of these traditional views of masculinity, male victims of harassment and assault may feel ashamed, emasculated, and confused about why their experiences do not align with society's view of masculinity. Research shows that male victims are more likely than female victims to struggle with anger and alcohol and drug abuse. Research has also found that male victims may face a higher risk of mental health problems, such as depression, than female victims. Furthermore, male victims may be less aware of resources available to help them report abuse and recover. They might feel that those resources are for female victims only.

People who support men and boys' participation in #MeToo believe excluding their stories only adds to the long-standing conventions that confuse, shame, and silence male victims. They argue that encouraging male victims to participate in #MeToo will help eliminate stigma and make disclosure easier for other victims.

Advocates for including male voices in the movement believe that doing so will help to advance the conversation about sexual harassment and assault in general. They also point out that including male voices helps people to consider the social and gender norms that enable abuse. The #MeToo movement has also called upon men and boys to engage in the conversation. The movement asks them to look at their behavior and take responsibility if they have perpetrated sexual misconduct.

LGBTQ AND #METOO

Another critique of the #MeToo movement is that it has focused too heavily on heterosexual experiences. This is despite the fact that members of the LGBTQ community experience disproportionate rates of sexual harassment and assault. The CDC and researchers studying assault and rape have found that lesbian women, gay men, and bisexual women and men face higher rates of sexual violence than heterosexual women and men. People who are transgender also face high rates of sexual harassment and abuse. In 2011, the National Transgender

People have worked hard to fight against transphobia, or the extreme dislike of people who are transgender or transsexual.

Discrimination survey found that 64 percent of transgender respondents had experienced sexual assault.[6]

Like many victims of sexual harassment and assault, members of the LGBTQ community face confusion, shame, and fear when considering talking about what happened to them. However, as is the case with other minority groups, LGBTQ victims also encounter unique layers of stereotyping and stigma. Stereotypes depict members of the LGBTQ community as promiscuous and hypersexual. There is also a misconception that unwanted advances cannot occur between people of the same sex. Among the most severe stereotypes is the myth that members of the LGBTQ community are pedophiles or sex offenders.

MORE TO THE
STORY

KEVIN SPACEY'S
ABUSE APOLOGY

Stereotypes became apparent in a celebrity #MeToo story involving actors Anthony Rapp and Kevin Spacey. The story emerged at the end of October 2017, shortly after news of the Weinstein scandal emerged. In the story, Rapp, who is openly gay, broke his silence on an experience with Spacey. He reported that Spacey made unwanted sexual advances toward him in 1986. At the time, Rapp was 14 and Spacey was 26.

In reaction to the news, Spacey tweeted a statement that ended with a disclosure about his sexual orientation: "I have loved and had romantic encounters with men throughout my life, and I choose now to live as a gay man. I want to deal with this honestly and openly and that starts with examining my own behavior." Spacey also noted that he did not remember the events Rapp reported, "But if I did behave then as he describes, I owe him the sincerest apology for what would have been deeply inappropriate drunken behavior."[7] Many people were quick to criticize Spacey's statement for promoting stereotypes and deflecting responsibility. People believed the statement placed blame for the assault on sexual orientation and on alcohol rather than on Spacey's individual choices.

Sexual assault survivors in the LGBTQ community may avoid breaking silence out of concern that reports will maintain those stereotypes, especially if the perpetrator is also a member of the LGBTQ community.

Advocates argue that the #MeToo movement should highlight survivor stories from the members of the LGBTQ community. They believe that doing so would help deconstruct stereotypes that silence victims. In addition, they think it would help eliminate the barriers that prevent victims from finding help.

Similarly to male victims of harassment and assault, LGBTQ victims have historically been excluded from the laws that protect against sexual harassment and abuse. For example, Title VII of the 1964 Civil Rights Act bans workplace harassment based on "race, color, religion, sex or national origin."[8] However, the language does not specifically mention sexual orientation or transgender rights. As of mid-2018, Congress had not expanded the wording of Title VII to include LGBTQ groups.

"MY TRANSNESS, QUEERNESS, AND BLACKNESS RENDER MY CLAIMS EVEN LESS BELIEVABLE IN A SOCIETY THAT VIEWS ME AS INHERENTLY DEVIANT."[9]

—RAQUEL WILLIS, NATIONAL ORGANIZER FOR THE TRANSGENDER LAW CENTER

The EEOC has often supported harassment complaints from members of the LGBTQ community, but without official wording in federal laws, courts and government officials sometimes overrule that support. States such as New York and California—as well as some cities such as Philadelphia, Pennsylvania—have laws that specifically protect the LGBTQ community from harassment, but other states do not.

LGBTQ survivors of sexual assault may also face discrimination when seeking help from law enforcement, health-care providers, social services, or crisis centers. A 2011 survey was done by the National Coalition of Anti-Violence Projects (NCAVP). It found that 85 percent of advocates working with NCAVP saw victims of intimate partner violence who had been turned away from those resources because of sexual orientation or gender identity.[10] An additional concern for LGBTQ survivors when reporting is the worry of revealing information about their gender or sexual orientation that they might not be ready to share. Activists believe featuring LGBTQ survivor stories in the #MeToo movement will help meet the needs of this community.

FROM THE HEADLINES

ACCUSATIONS AGAINST CRISTINA GARCIA

Cristina Garcia is a Democratic assemblywoman in California and head of California's Legislative Women's Caucus. Garcia had been a leading voice in the #MeToo movement. *Time* included her picture in a photo montage of silence breakers alongside their 2017 Person of the Year article. In February 2018, male colleagues and subordinates reported her for misconduct, which involved sexually explicit comments and groping. The allegations against Garcia made headlines and raised questions of hypocrisy in the movement, female perpetrators, false accusations, and due process. Garcia denies the claims. She believes they are motivated by disagreement with her political positions. Nonetheless, she took a voluntary, unpaid leave of absence from her position to allow an investigation to take place. The initial investigation cleared her of the charge.

Cristina Garcia was elected to the California State Assembly in 2012.

CHAPTER EIGHT

THE PAST
AND FUTURE

I n early 2018, *Vanity Fair* published an article by
Monica Lewinsky. Lewinsky was involved in a sex
scandal with President Bill Clinton during the 1990s
when she was an intern at the White House. The affair
between Clinton and Lewinsky came to light when
Clinton was under investigation for other allegations
of sexual harassment and financial misconduct. Even
though Clinton was the subject of the investigation,
the media, politicians, and public opinion vilified
Lewinsky. They painted her as promiscuous, unstable,
and opportunistic. Clinton went on to serve out
the rest of his presidential term with high approval
ratings. Meanwhile, Lewinsky struggled with bullying,
unemployment, and post-traumatic stress disorder even

Monica Lewinsky was demonized by the media after the Clinton scandal.
Today, she is an antibullying advocate.

INCIDENCE OF FALSE ACCUSATION

Concerns about false reporting have arisen in #MeToo conversations. A review of research by the NSVRC found that between 2 and 10 percent of sexual assault reports are false.[2] According to the NSVRC, that range may overestimate the problem because many agencies incorrectly label reports as false. For example, some agencies believe that a delay in reporting or an inconsistency in the victim's memory means the report is false. However, false reports occur in only a small percentage of cases. For people who are falsely accused, there can be serious consequences, such as losing their job or reputation or facing a hostile work environment. People who have been falsely accused emphasize that there should be thorough investigations before enforcing punishment, as well as clear consequences for people who make false accusations.

20 years after the scandal. The case tainted her personal and professional reputations and dominated her identity.

The *Vanity Fair* article is entitled "Emerging from 'The House of Gaslight' in the Age of #MeToo."[1] The term *gaslight* has appeared frequently in the #MeToo movement, and it refers to tactics used by powerful people to discredit a victim. Those tactics cause victims to doubt that abuse occurred, to question their memories and perceptions, and to blame themselves.

Lewinsky has consistently reported that Clinton did not rape or sexually assault her. However, in her new essay, Lewinsky argued that Clinton's actions constituted an abuse of power. When the affair occurred, Lewinsky was an intern in her early twenties. Clinton was her boss, president of the United States, married, and 27 years older than Lewinsky. Given those differences in power, Lewinsky writes, "I now see how problematic it was that the two of us even got to a place where there was a question of consent. Instead, the road that led there was littered with inappropriate abuse of authority, station, and privilege."[3] Lewinsky explains that the #MeToo movement provides a new lens for understanding both her inappropriate affair with Clinton and the abuse, scapegoating, and gaslighting that took place in the ensuing scandal.

Lewinsky's essay touches on a topic that has received much discussion in the #MeToo movement: what should become of the legacies of great men and women who perpetrate sexual harassment and abuse? The question circulates around perpetrators from the past as well as those in the present.

RECONSIDERING PAST AND PRESENT LEGACIES

Many influential people from the past, such as the painter Pablo Picasso, the filmmaker Alfred Hitchcock, and the rapper Tupac Shakur, have been accused of sexual harassment and abusive behavior. At the same time, their work has influenced culture in significant ways. Some people believe it is possible to separate work contributions from the details of a person's life. According to this point of view, work should be judged on its merit rather than on biographical details. Other people point out that erasing past contributions eliminates the opportunity to think critically about history, culture, and progress.

These conversations have focused on the present too. Not only have several high-profile figures lost their jobs—companies and projects have wiped away traces of their contributions. For example, after news of actor Kevin Spacey's sexual misconduct broke, director Ridley Scott refilmed scenes in the movie *All the Money in the World* to cut Spacey from the film just weeks before it premiered. Scott replaced Spacey with actor Christopher Plummer even though Spacey's performance had already gathered talk of an Oscar

"I CAN'T HELP BUT WONDER THAT IF WE REMOVED ALL THE BOOKS AND ART CREATED BY MEN WHO'VE ALSO DONE DESPICABLE THINGS IN THEIR LIVES, OUR SHELVES AND WALLS WOULD BE MIGHTY EMPTY."[4]

—MARY ANNETTE PEMBER, JOURNALIST

Netflix fired Kevin Spacey from the television show *House of Cards* after accusations against him surfaced.

nomination. When harassment and abuse is severe, many people feel that such drastic actions are justified. Even in cases that are less severe, some people call for zero tolerance policies against perpetrators. However, other people raise questions about the rush to judgment and where to draw the line when it comes to firing people and erasing their legacies.

These debates gain additional layers when people consider issues such as the time and severity of the sexual misconduct. People question whether others should face personal and professional consequences for noncriminal harassment done years ago. They also ask whether there should be different consequences for different types of harassment and abuse. For example, should people who tell sexist jokes be given a second chance to preserve their job and legacy while someone who gropes a colleague receives no such chance? These are all questions people have asked in the context of the #MeToo movement.

MOVING FORWARD WITH A FOCUS ON VICTIMS

Many people in the #MeToo movement have argued that victims' voices are lost in the midst of questions about perpetrators' legacies. To move forward, they suggest approaches that focus less on the perpetrators and more on changing the cultural, professional, and political systems that allow abuse.

One suggestion calls for more equality in professional representation and pay. For example, in an Academy Award speech after winning best actress in 2018, Frances McDormand urged her colleagues to demand inclusion riders on their future movie projects. Inclusion riders are contract clauses that ensure gender and racial diversity among the cast and crew who work on films. For instance, an inclusion rider clause could require that 50 percent of cast and crew positions be filled by women and minorities.

Calls for equal pay refer to the long-standing pay gaps that affect women and minorities. In terms of hourly and yearly earnings, white men make more money than black men, Hispanic men, and women of all races. Even when men and women hold the same positions and do the same kind of work, men earn more than women in many professions. Journalist Susan Antilla claims that the pay gap supports a culture of inequality. Advocates in the #MeToo movement argue that workplace diversity, equality in professional opportunities, and equal pay for equal work will eliminate some of the power discrepancies that allow harassment and abuse to occur.

CAMPUS SEXUAL VIOLENCE

Sexual assault on college and university campuses is a widespread problem. Researchers for the Association of American Universities (AAU) indicate that about 23 percent of female undergraduate students and 5 percent of male undergraduate students are victims of sexual assault.[5] The AAU as well as the US Department of Justice point out that judging the accuracy of those statistics is difficult because underreporting occurs frequently. Reasons for high rates of sexual violence and low rates of reporting include the unique structure of social life on college campuses. The social life in these places frequently includes alcohol and drug use as well as peer pressure. Some claim that these factors create a rape culture on campuses. This means that the culture makes sexual misconduct appear normal. Many advocates in the #MeToo movement believe that college campuses are an ideal place to change toxic cultures by encouraging broad educational opportunities and conversations about consent, sexual violence, empathy, and respect.

Other initiatives involve legal and educational action. For example, congressional lawmakers introduced the Me Too Congress Act in November 2017. The act would make reporting sexual harassment easier for people working in Congress, including interns and pages. It would also eliminate the requirement that victims sign nondisclosure agreements. Lawmakers have presented similar legislative ideas for private businesses. These ideas aim to stop the silencing and cover-ups that frequently accompany reports of harassment and abuse.

#MeToo supporters have suggested increasing efforts, such as Time's Up, that give victims practical legal resources and financial help. There has also been a focus on expanding education within schools, families, and communities to change the culture. Programs such as LiveRespect, Coaching Boys into Men, and Project Speak Out partner with schools to combat gender stereotypes and sexual violence. For instance, Project Speak Out teaches high school students a "direct, distract, and delegate" method.[6] The method helps teens understand how to stop harassment by getting directly involved, creating a distraction, and seeking help from adults.

George Garrison, a student athlete at a New Jersey high school, said the program helped him intervene when he heard peers making sexual comments about girls' bodies.

Citing examples like Garrison's, activists believe that #MeToo efforts will help bring about widespread cultural and systemic changes for survivors of sexual harassment and abuse. However, others wonder whether the movement's momentum will continue in a society that is used to quick changes in trending topics. Still others question whether the various debates on #MeToo's goals and reach will fracture the movement. As people in the #MeToo movement look at the legacies of those who have harassed and abused, they also consider the movement's future and its legacy.

People of all genders have shown support for the #MeToo movement.

ESSENTIAL
FACTS

MAJOR EVENTS

- On October 5, 2017, the *New York Times* ran a story exposing producer Harvey Weinstein as a serial sexual predator. Ten days later, on October 15, actress Alyssa Milano tweeted, "If you've been sexually harassed or assaulted write 'me too' as a reply to this tweet." The tweet was a direct response to the Weinstein story. It gained millions of posts and replies within 24 hours.

- On December 6, 2017, *Time* magazine named the silence breakers as the Person of the Year. The Person of the Year title is given annually to a person or group who has made a significant impact on the year's events.

KEY PLAYERS

- Carmita Wood and researchers in Cornell University's Human Affairs Program devised and popularized the term *sexual harassment* in 1975 to convey the wide spectrum of inappropriate comments, looks, jokes, touches, and attacks women encounter.

- Mechelle Vinson won the first Supreme Court case to find sexual harassment to be a form of employment discrimination in 1986.

- Tarana Burke created the Me Too campaign in 2006 to assist sexual violence victims in brown and black communities.

- McKayla Maroney tweeted #MeToo on October 18, 2017, bringing attention to sexual abuse against minors.

IMPACT ON SOCIETY

Sexual harassment and assault is widespread in US society. Experiencing sexual harassment or assault impacts a person's ability to lead a healthy, productive life. As silence breakers have revealed their experiences, powerful people have lost their jobs and historical legacies have come under scrutiny. The #MeToo movement challenges deeply ingrained social norms, gender roles, and power structures that enable sexual misconduct. As a result of the movement, people have reevaluated how they engage with others at work, in relationships, and in public spaces.

QUOTE

"If all the women who have been sexually harassed or assaulted wrote 'Me too' as a status, we might give people a sense of the magnitude of the problem."

—Alyssa Milano, 2017

GLOSSARY

CONSENT

Agreement in or permission for something.

DISCLOSURE

The revelation of previously unknown, usually sensitive, information.

LGBTQ

An acronym used to describe nonheterosexual people: lesbian, gay, bisexual, transgender, and queer or questioning.

SEXUAL ABUSE

A general term for unwanted or criminal sexual contact, often used in reference to minors or intimate relationships.

SEXUAL ASSAULT

A general term for a criminal sexual act.

SEXUAL HARASSMENT

Unwanted verbal or physical behavior that is sexual or gender based.

SEXUAL ORIENTATION

A person's identity in relation to the gender(s) they find sexually attractive.

SILENCE BREAKER

Someone who publicly reveals an incident of sexual harassment or assault.

VICTIM BLAMING

Placing responsibility for sexual misconduct on the victim rather than the perpetrator.

ADDITIONAL
RESOURCES

SELECTED BIBLIOGRAPHY

Berebitsky, Julie. *Sex and the Office: A History of Gender, Power, and Desire.* Yale UP, 2012.

Kearl, Holly. *Stop Street Harassment: Making Public Places Safe and Welcoming for Women.* Praeger, 2010.

Wright, Erik Olin. *American Society: How It Really Works.* Norton, 2015.

FURTHER READINGS

Harris, Duchess. *Sexism and Race.* Abdo, 2018.

Harris, Duchess. *Sexism at Work.* Abdo, 2018.

Rissman, Rebecca. *Rape Culture and Sexual Violence.* Abdo, 2018.

ONLINE RESOURCES

To learn more about the silence breakers and the #MeToo movement, visit **abdobooklinks.com**. These links are routinely monitored and updated to provide the most current information available.

MORE INFORMATION

For more information on this subject, contact or visit the following organizations:

National Women's Law Center
11 Dupont Circle NW, #800
Washington, DC 20036
202-588-5180
nwlc.org
The National Women's Law Center administers the Time's Up Legal
Defense Fund. The center connects victims with legal and financial
resources and educates the general public about issues affecting the
rights of women and girls.

US Equal Employment Opportunity Commission
131 M Street NE
Washington, DC 20507
202-663-4900
eeoc.gov
The Equal Employment Opportunity Commission (EEOC) is the federal
agency that oversees matters of workplace harassment, including sexual
harassment.

SOURCE
NOTES

CHAPTER 1. THE STORY OF #METOO

1. Tarana Burke. "The Inception." *Just Be*, n.d., justbeinc.wixsite.com. Accessed 15 Aug. 2018.

2. "You Are Not Alone." *Me Too*, n.d., metoomvmt.org. Accessed 15 Aug. 2018.

3. @Alyssa_Milano. "If you've been sexually harassed or assaulted write 'me too' as a reply to this tweet." *Twitter*, 15 Oct. 2017, 1:21 p.m., twitter.com. Accessed 15 Aug. 2018.

4. Cassandra Santiago and Doug Criss. "An Activist, a Little Girl, and the Heartbreaking Origin of 'Me Too.'" *CNN*, 17 Oct. 2017, cnn.com. Accessed 15 Aug. 2018.

5. Madeline Berg. "After Expulsion from the Academy, Here Are All of Weinstein's 81 Oscar Wins." *Forbes*, 14 Oct. 2017, forbes.com. Accessed 15 Aug. 2018.

6. Yohana Desta and Hillary Busis. "These Are the Women Who Have Accused Harvey Weinstein of Sexual Harassment and Assault." *Vanity Fair*, 12 Oct. 2018, vanityfair.com. Accessed 15 Aug. 2018.

7. Jodi Kantor and Megan Twohey. "Harvey Weinstein Paid Off Sexual Harassment Accusers for Decades." *New York Times*, 5 Oct. 2017, nytimes.com. Accessed 15 Aug. 2018.

8. Nadja Sayej. "Alyssa Milano on the #MeToo Movement: 'We're Not Going to Stand for It Any More." *Guardian*, 1 Dec. 2017, theguardian.com. Accessed 15 Aug. 2018.

9. Stephanie Zacharek, et al. "The Silence Breakers." *Time*, 18 Dec. 2017, time.com. Accessed 15 Aug. 2018.

10. Carly Mallenbaum. "A Complete List of the 60 Bill Cosby Accusers and Their Reactions to the Guilty Verdict." *USA Today*, 27 Apr. 2018, usatoday.com. Accessed 15 Aug. 2018.

CHAPTER 2. BEFORE #METOO

1. Erik Olin Wright. *American Society: How It Really Works*. Norton, 2015. 29.

2. "Title VII of the Civil Rights Act of 1964." *US Equal Opportunity Commission*, n.d., eeoc.gov. Accessed 15 Aug. 2018.

3. Fred Strebeigh. *Equal: Women Reshape American Law*. Norton, 2009. 219.

4. Glenn C. Altschuler. *Cornell: A History, 1940–2015*. Cornell UP, 2014. 146.

5. Sarah Mearhoff. "#MeToo: Fight against Workplace Sexual Harassment Began at Cornell in 1975." *Ithaca Journal*, 21 Feb. 2018, ithacajournal.com. Accessed 15 Aug. 2018.

6. Anita Hill. "Opening Statement to the Senate Judiciary Committee." *American Rhetoric*, 11 Oct. 1991, americanrhetoric.com. Accessed 15 Aug. 2018.

7. Elizabeth Blair. "Women Are Speaking Up about Harassment and Abuse, but Why Now?" *NPR*, 27 Oct. 2017, npr.org. Accessed 15 Aug. 2018.

8. Leigh Gilmore. *Tainted Witness: Why We Don't Believe What Women Say about Their Lives*. Columbia UP, 2017. 33.

9. Gilmore, *Tainted Witness*, 28.

10. R. W. Apple Jr. "The Thomas Confirmation; Senate Confirms Thomas, 52–48, Ending Week of Bitter Battle; 'Time for Healing,' Judge Says." *New York Times*, 16 Oct. 1991, nytimes.com. Accessed 15 Aug. 2018.

11. "The Year of the Woman, 1992." *History, Art & Archives*, n.d., history.house.gov. Accessed 15 Aug. 2018.

12. Julie Berebitsky. *Sex and the Office: A History of Gender, Power, and Desire*. Yale UP, 2012. 4.

13. Robert Farley. "Trump's Rare Apology." *FactCheck.org*, 12 Dec. 2017, factcheck.org. Accessed 15 Aug. 2018.

14. Claire Cain Miller. "#MeToo—How Social Media Gives Women a Voice." *WRAL Tech Wire*, 12 Feb. 2018, wraltechwire.com. Accessed 15 Aug. 2018.

15. Anne Ursu. "Sexual Harassment in the Children's Book Industry." *Medium*, 7 Feb. 2018, medium.com. Accessed 15 Aug. 2018.

16. Doug Stanglin. "Cryptic Tweet from Stormy Daniels' Lawyer Hints at Photos Tied to Alleged Trump Affair." *USA Today*, 23 Mar. 2018, usatoday.com. Accessed 15 Aug. 2018.

CHAPTER 3. #METOO IN THE WORKPLACE

1. Julie Berebitsky. *Sex and the Office: A History of Gender, Power, and Desire*. Yale UP, 2012. 2.

2. Louise Radnofsky. "Poll: 48% of Employed Women Say They Have Been Sexually Harassed at Work." *Wall Street Journal*, 30 Oct. 2017, wsj.com. Accessed 15 Aug. 2018.

3. Jodi Kantor and Megan Twohey. "Harvey Weinstein Paid Off Sexual Harassment Accusers for Decades." *New York Times*, 5 Oct. 2017, nytimes.com. Accessed 15 Aug. 2018.

4. Peter Balonon-Rosen and Kimberly Adams. "One in 7 Men Say They've Been Sexually Harassed at Work." *Marketplace*, 9 Mar. 2018, marketplace.org. Accessed 15 Aug. 2018.

5. "Sexual Harassment." *US Equal Opportunity Employment Commission*, n.d., eeoc.gov. Accessed 15 Aug. 2018.

6. Andrea Park. "#MeToo Reaches 85 Countries with 1.7M Tweets." *CBS News*, 24 Oct. 2017, cbsnews.com. Accessed 15 Aug. 2018.

7. "Nearly 235 Million Women Worldwide Lack Legal Protections from Sexual Harassment at Work." *UCLA*, 26 Oct. 2017, ph.ucla.edu. Accessed 15 Aug. 2018.

8. Sarah Mearhoff. "#MeToo: Fight against Workplace Sexual Harassment Began at Cornell in 1975." *Ithaca Journal*, 21 Feb. 2018, ithacajournal.com. Accessed 15 Aug. 2018.

9. Yuki Noguchi. "Low-Wage Workers Say #MeToo Movement Is a Chance for Change." *NPR*, 6 Feb. 2018, npr.org. Accessed 15 Aug. 2018.

10. Brad Smith. "What Microsoft Learned from Our #MeToo Moment." *Washington Post*, 22 Dec. 2017, washingtonpost.com. Accessed 15 Aug. 2018.

11. Maya Kosoff. "The 'Boys' Club' Mentality Is Still Alive': How Millennial Women Are Combatting the Gender-Pay Gap." *Vanity Fair*, 9 Apr. 2018, vanityfair.com. Accessed 15 Aug. 2018.

12. Heather McLaughlin et al. "The Cost of Sexual Harassment." *Gender & Society*, 7 June 2017, gendersociety.wordpress.com. Accessed 15 Aug. 2018.

13. "Graham, Gillibrand Announce Bipartisan Legislation to Help Prevent Sexual Harassment in the Workplace." *Lindsey Graham*, 6 Dec. 2017, lgraham.senate.gov. Accessed 15 Aug. 2018.

CHAPTER 4. THE MOVEMENT OUTSIDE OF WORK

1. Sharon G. Smith et al. "National Intimate Partner and Sexual Violence Survey: 2015 Data Brief." *Centers for Disease Control and Prevention*, May 2018, cdc.gov. Accessed 15 Aug. 2018.

SOURCE NOTES
CONTINUED

2. Alia E. Dastagir. "The #MeToo Survivors We Forgot." *USA Today*, 19 Apr. 2018, usatoday.com. Accessed 15 Aug. 2018.

3. "Street Harassment." *Advocates for Human Rights*, Aug. 2013, stopvaw.org. Accessed 15 Aug. 2018.

4. Holly Kearl. "Unsafe and Harassed in Public Spaces: A National Street Harassment Report." *Stop Street Harassment*, Spring 2014, stopstreetharassment.org. Accessed 15 Aug. 2018.

5. Hannan Adely. "After #MeToo, a Program Aims to Make Boys a Part of the Solution." *North Jersey*, 18 Feb. 2018, northjersey.com. Accessed 15 Aug. 2018.

6. Alanna Vagianos. "These Are the Explicit Things Men Say to Women on the Street." *Huffington Post*, 1 Dec. 2017, huffingtonpost.com. Accessed 15 Aug. 2018.

CHAPTER 5. MINORS IN THE MOVEMENT

1. Tracy Connor. "McKayla Maroney Says Dr. Larry Nassar Molested Her in #MeToo Post." *NBC News*, 18 Oct. 2017, nbcnews.com. Accessed 15 Aug. 2018.

2. "Larry Nassar Jailed for Another 40 to 125 Years." *BBC News*, 5 Feb. 2018, bbc.com. Accessed 15 Aug. 2018.

3. "Raising Awareness about Sexual Abuse." *NSOPW*, n.d., nsopw.gov. Accessed 15 Aug. 2018.

4. "Perpetrators of Sexual Violence: Statistics." *RAINN*, n.d., rainn.org. Accessed 15 Aug. 2018.

5. Dorothy L. Espelage et al. "Bullying, Sexual, and Dating Violence Trajectories from Early to Late Adolescence." *National Institute of Justice*, 21 Apr. 2014, ncjrs.gov. Accessed 15 Aug. 2018.

6. Tracy Connor. "Gymnastics Doctor Larry Nassar Faces Sex-Abuse Accusers in Court." *NBC News*, 12 May 2017, nbcnews.com. Accessed 15 Aug. 2018.

7. "Child Sexual Abuse Facts." *Children's Assessment Center*, n.d., cachouston.org. Accessed 15 Aug. 2018.

8. Tom Lutz. "Victim Impact Statements against Larry Nassar: 'I Thought I Was Going to Die." *Guardian*, 24 Jan. 2018, theguardian.com. Accessed 15 Aug. 2018.

9. Lulu Garcia-Navarro. "Nassar Testimony Brings One Sexual Abuse Survivor Sadness—And Then Some Relief." *NPR*, 21 Jan. 2018, npr.org. Accessed 15 Aug. 2018.

CHAPTER 6. THE #METOO MOVEMENT AND RACE

1. Audra Burch. "The #MeToo Moment: After Alabama, Black Women Wonder, What's Next?" *New York Times*, 14 Dec. 2017, nytimes.com. Accessed 15 Aug. 2018.

2. Jessica Prois and Carolina Moreno. "The #MeToo Movement Looks Different for Women of Color. Here Are 10 Stories." *Huffington Post*, 2 Jan. 2018, huffingtonpost.com. Accessed 15 Aug. 2018.

3. "Tribal Affairs." *US Department of Justice*, 31 July 2018, justice.gov. Accessed 15 Aug. 2018.

4. Mary Annette Pember. "Sherman Alexie and the Longest Running #MeToo Movement in History." *Rewire News*, 2 Mar. 2018, rewire.news. Accessed 15 Aug. 2018.

5. Pember, "Sherman Alexie."

6. Pember, "Sherman Alexie."

7. Jim DeRogatis. "The Woman Who Said R. Kelly Abused Her Refuses to Be Silenced." *BuzzFeed News*, 13 Mar. 2018, buzzfeednews.com. Accessed 15 Aug. 2018.

CHAPTER 7. GENDER AND SEXUAL ORIENTATION

1. @Alyssa_Milano. "If you've been sexually harassed or assaulted write 'me too' as a reply to this tweet." *Twitter*, 15 Oct. 2017, 1:21 p.m., twitter.com. Accessed 15 Aug. 2018.

2. Meredith G. F. Worthen. *Sexual Deviances and Society: A Sociological Examination*. Routledge, 2016. 335.

3. Paget Norton. "The Problem with Men Saying #MeToo." *Good Men Project*, 24 Oct. 2017, goodmenproject.com. Accessed 15 Aug. 2018.

4. Peter Balonon-Rosen and Kimberly Adams. "One in 7 Men Say They've Been Sexually Harassed at Work." *Marketplace*, 9 Mar. 2018, marketplace.org. Accessed 15 Aug. 2018.

5. Jim Garamone. "Experts: Males Also Are Victims of Sexual Assault." *US Department of Defense*, 20 Feb. 2015, defense.gov. Accessed 15 Aug. 2018.

6. Jamie M. Grant et al. "Injustice at Every Turn." *Task Force*, n.d., thetaskforce.org. Accessed 15 Aug. 2018.

7. @KevinSpacey. "I have a lot of respect and admiration for Anthony Rapp as an actor." *Twitter*, 26 Oct. 2017, 9:00 p.m., twitter.com. Accessed 15 Aug. 2018.

8. Alan Feuer. "Justice Department Says Rights Law Doesn't Protect Gays." *New York Times*, 27 July 2017, nytimes.com. Accessed 15 Aug. 2018.

9. Raquel Willis. "#UsToo: We Must Expand the Conversation on Sexual Violence." *INTO*, 23 Oct. 2017, intomore.com. Accessed 15 Aug. 2018.

10. "Sexual Assault and the LGBTQ Community." *Human Rights Campaign*, n.d., hrc.org. Accessed 15 Aug. 2018.

CHAPTER 8. THE PAST AND FUTURE

1. Monica Lewinsky. "Monica Lewinsky: Emerging from 'The House of Gaslight' in the Age of #MeToo." *Vanity Fair*, Mar. 2018, vanityfair.com. Accessed 15 Aug. 2018.

2. "False Reporting." *National Sexual Violence Resource Center*, n.d., nsvrc.org. Accessed 15 Aug. 2018.

3. Lewinsky, "Emerging from 'The House of Gaslight.'"

4. Mary Annette Pember. "Sherman Alexie and the Longest Running #MeToo Movement in History." *Rewire News*, 2 Mar. 2018, rewire.news. Accessed 15 Aug. 2018.

5. "Campus Sexual Violence: Statistics." *RAINN*, n.d., rainn.org. Accessed 15 Aug. 2018.

6. Hannan Adely. "After #MeToo, a Program Aims to Make Boys a Part of the Solution." *North Jersey*, 18 Feb. 2018, northjersey.com. Accessed 15 Aug. 2018.

INDEX

Academy Award, 8, 96
Academy of Motion Picture Arts and
    Sciences, 10
Advocates for Human Rights, 50
Affleck, Ben, 8
Alexie, Sherman, 74

Batali, Mario, 11, 40
Black Women's Blueprint, 74
Burke, Tarana, 4, 6, 13, 33, 77

Centers for Disease Control and
    Prevention (CDC), 48, 59, 83
Chastain, Jessica, 14
Civil Rights Act of 1991, 28
Clifford, Stephanie "Stormy Daniels,"
    34
Clinton, Bill, 29, 31, 90, 92–93
Clinton, Hillary, 29, 31
Cohen, Michael, 34
Constand, Andrea, 16
Cornell University, 21–22
Cosby, Bill, 16

Damon, Matt, 8
Dantzscher, Jamie, 66
Denhollander, Rachael, 66

Ending the Forced Arbitration of
    Sexual Harassment Act, 44
Equal Employment Opportunity
    Commission (EEOC), 20–21,
    23–25, 28, 39, 87

Farquhar, Lita, 41–42
Fowler, Susan, 32–33
Franken, Al, 11

Garcia, Cristina, 88
Geddert, John, 62

hashtag, 13, 16, 33, 36, 76
Hill, Anita, 24–28
Hitchcock, Alfred, 93

Judd, Ashley, 14

Kelly, Robert Sylvester "R. Kelly,"
    76–77
Kelly-Cabrera, Zahira, 71

Lauer, Matt, 7, 10–11
Lawrence, Jennifer, 8
Levine, James, 11, 40
Lewinsky, Monica, 31, 90, 92–93
LGBTQ, 80, 83–84, 86–87

Maroney, McKayla, 56, 58, 67
McDaniel, Boyce, 21
McDormand, Frances, 96
McGowan, Rose, 13
Meritor Savings Bank v. Vinson, 24
Michigan State University (MSU), 56, 63, 64–65
Milano, Alyssa, 6–7, 12–13, 78
Miramax, 7
Moore, Jacob, 66
Mujeres Latinas en Acción, 74

Nassar, Larry, 11, 56, 58–60, 62–65, 67
National Sexual Violence Resource Center (NSVRC), 14, 92
New York Times, 7–8, 10, 12, 23
1964 Civil Rights Act, 20, 28, 86
Nineteenth Amendment, 18
nondisclosure agreements, 12, 34, 98

Pace, Jerhonda, 76–77
Paltrow, Gwyneth, 8
Pember, Mary Annette, 73–74, 94
Person of the Year, 14, 78, 88
Picasso, Pablo, 93

rape, 8, 10, 13, 16, 24, 38, 41, 49, 54, 71–72, 80–81, 83, 92, 97
Rape, Abuse, and Incest National Network, 50
Rapp, Anthony, 85
Rose, Charlie, 40
Roupenian, Kristen, 54

Shakur, Tupac, 94
Spacey, Kevin, 11, 85, 94
Stephens, Kyle, 65–67
street harassment, 46, 50–53, 55, 61
Supreme Court, 24–26

Thomas, Clarence, 24–26
Thomashow, Amanda, 63–64
Time's Up, 45, 77, 98
Tony Awards, 8
Trump, Donald, 29–31, 34
Twitter, 6, 12, 56, 67, 78, 85

Uber, 32
USA Gymnastics, 64–65

Weinstein, Harvey, 7–8, 10–14, 36, 76–77, 85
Weinstein Company, 7, 38
whisper networks, 14
Women's March, 30, 33
Wood, Carmita, 21–23, 28, 40
Working Women United, 22–23
workplace sexual harassment, 36, 38–45
WORLD Policy Analysis Center, 39

ABOUT THE
AUTHORS

DUCHESS HARRIS, JD, PHD

Professor Harris is the chair of the American Studies department at Macalester College and curator of the Duchess Harris Collection of ABDO books. She is the author and coauthor of recently released ABDO books including *Hidden Human Computers: The Black Women of NASA*, *Black Lives Matter*, and *Race and Policing*.

Before working with ABDO, she authored several other books on the topics of race, culture, and American history. She served as an associate editor for *Litigation News*, the American Bar Association Section of Litigation's quarterly flagship publication, and was the first editor in chief of *Law Raza*, an interactive online journal covering race and the law, published at William Mitchell College of Law. She has earned a PhD in American Studies from the University of Minnesota and a JD from William Mitchell College of Law.

REBECCA MORRIS

Rebecca Morris has a PhD in English from Texas A&M University. She is the author of nonfiction books for students. Morris also writes literature guides for education websites.